DOCKSIDE

STAGE 1

BOOK 7

NOT GOOD, TASHA!

Philippa Bateman

RISING STARS

Look at this!
Mum got JJ an iPod.

Did you sit on it?

I put my foot
on it.

This is not good, Tasha!

Put it in JJ's hoodie.
Then hook it on the door.

No ...

Put a book on it.
THE BIG HEAVY BOOK

No ...

Look, it's JJ. He will see his iPod.

This is not good!

Are you ok? You look odd.

Tasha took your iPod. Look at it.

But look, **this** is my iPod.
Mum got that for **you**!

This is **not** good, Tasha!